GOOGLE SLIDES

FOR BEGINNERS

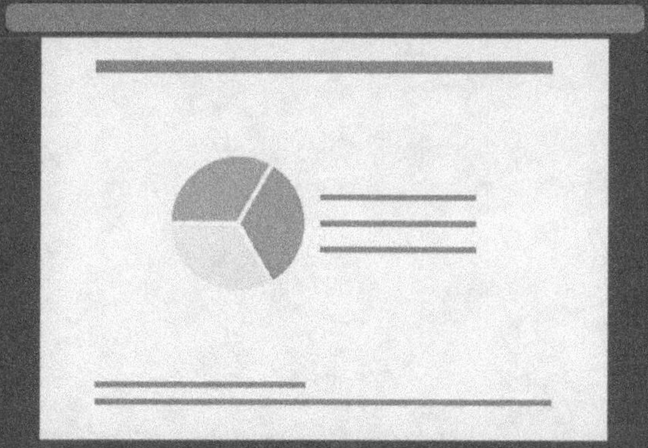

The Complete Step-By-Step Guide To Learning How To Create, Edit, Share And Collaborate On presentations

GOOGLE SLIDES FOR BEGINNERS

The Complete Step-By-Step Guide To Learning How To Create, Edit, Share And Collaborate On presentations

GOOGLE SLIDES FOR BEGINNERS: THE COMPLETE STEP-BY-STEP GUIDE TO LEARNING HOW TO CREATE, EDIT, SHARE AND COLLABORATE ON PRESENTATIONS

First edition. November 27, 2023.

Written by Voltaire Lumiere.

TABLE OF CONTENTS

CHAPTER 1
INTRODUCTION TO GOOGLE SLIDES

- **Understanding the Basics**

In the realm of Google Slides, the canvas becomes a digital playground, a space where creativity dances with functionality. At its core, Google Slides is a cloud-based presentation software that redefines the boundaries of collaborative storytelling. It's not just about slides; it's about the seamless fusion of ideas and the fluidity of visual narratives.

Here, your canvas isn't confined by physical borders. The power of the cloud allows your creations to transcend the limitations of a single device. Your ideas live in the digital ether, ready to be shaped, reshaped, and refined at a moment's notice.

Each click, each drag, echoes across the vastness of the cloud, inviting collaboration. The Basics lay the foundation, introducing you to the language of slides, the art of arrangement, and the subtle dance of text and imagery.

Within this realm, a slide is not just a static image; it's a dynamic scene waiting to unfold. Understanding the Basics means deciphering the language of layouts, comprehending the nuanced art of font selection, and embracing the whitespace that breathes life into your creation.

As you navigate the interface, notice the simplicity that belies its power. The ribbon of options invites exploration—a palette of tools, each with a purpose. The Basic commands become second nature, orchestrating your symphony of ideas effortlessly.

Here, you don't merely create slides; you craft an experience. Understanding the Basics isn't a lesson; it's an initiation into a realm where pixels carry the weight of stories, and the digital canvas becomes a conduit for your imagination.

In this space, your ideas take flight, unrestricted by the conventional boundaries of a presentation. It's not just about slides; it's about the fusion of simplicity and sophistication, where the Basics lay the groundwork for your journey into the expansive universe of Google Slides.

- **Why Use Google Slides?**

Unlocking the "Why" behind Google Slides unveils a world where collaboration, accessibility, and dynamic creativity converge. Google Slides isn't just a presentation tool; it's a gateway to a new paradigm of communication and engagement.

At its core, Google Slides breathes life into your ideas by offering a canvas that transcends physical limitations. The cloud-based nature of Google Slides means your presentations are no longer confined to a single device or location. They exist in a realm of accessibility, allowing you to create, edit, and present seamlessly, whether you're at your desk or on the go.

The collaborative heartbeat of Google Slides sets it apart. No longer is the creative process a solitary endeavor; it's a symphony of minds working in unison. Real-time collaboration transforms the creation process into a dynamic dialogue, where ideas are shared, refined, and elevated collectively.

Why Google Slides? Because it's a bridge between individual brilliance and collaborative genius. It empowers teams to contribute, edit, and shape the narrative in real-time, fostering a sense of unity and shared ownership.

Moreover, Google Slides dismantles the barriers of traditional presentation software. It's not confined to a specific operating system, ensuring a universal language for communication. Your presentations become an inclusive experience, accessible to anyone with an internet connection, regardless of their device or location.

In this realm, engagement is not a passive act but an interactive dance. Why Google Slides? Because it introduces a level of interactivity that transcends the static nature of conventional presentations. Embedded videos, live polls, and audience participation features transform your presentation into an immersive experience, captivating your audience and leaving a lasting impression.

Ultimately, the allure of Google Slides lies in its ability to transform the mundane into the extraordinary. It's not just a tool; it's a catalyst for dynamic storytelling, fostering collaboration, accessibility, and creativity in a way that redefines the very essence of presentations.

- **Getting Started with Google Slides**

Embarking on the journey of "Getting Started with Google Slides" opens the door to a realm where simplicity meets boundless creative potential. Here, initiation isn't just a series of steps; it's an invitation to a platform designed to amplify your ideas and streamline your creative process.

As you take your first steps into Google Slides, the welcoming embrace of a clean, intuitive interface greets you. The simplicity is deliberate—a deliberate design to ensure that your focus remains on your ideas, not the intricacies of the tool itself.

The first encounter with the "+ New" button is the inception of your creative odyssey. A click, a canvas—blank, yet pregnant with possibility. Your journey begins with selecting a template, a visual scaffold that aligns with the essence of your message. From the simplicity of a blank slate to the guidance of predefined themes, the choice is yours.

Mastering the art of slides is akin to arranging the pages of a visual story. The toolbar becomes your artistic palette, offering an array of options—shapes, text boxes, images. Each click adds a layer to your narrative, and as you explore, you'll find that arranging, aligning, and grouping elements become second nature.

But it's not just about static elements. The magic of Google Slides lies in the fluidity of motion. Transitions are not just passages between slides; they are the heartbeat of your presentation. They add rhythm, guiding your audience through a seamless flow of ideas.

Getting Started isn't merely about understanding the tools; it's about grasping the essence of collaboration. The "Share" button isn't just a feature; it's an open invitation to co-create. Collaboration is woven into the fabric of Google Slides, allowing you to invite others to view, comment, and contribute in real-time.

Your initiation into Google Slides isn't a conventional tutorial; it's an immersion into a space where ideas materialize effortlessly. Getting Started isn't a prelude; it's the first chapter of a creative journey where the canvas is boundless, and your ideas are set free to flourish.

- **Overview of the User Interface**

Navigating the "Overview of the User Interface" in Google Slides is akin to embarking on a visual expedition, where every element is purposefully placed to enhance your creative journey.

The interface is a landscape—a canvas in itself—crafted for intuitive exploration.

At first glance, the simplicity of the interface is striking. The top bar, a digital horizon, hosts the command center—your access point to the tools that shape your presentation. Here, the familiar icons beckon: the floppy disk, a guardian of your creations; the "+," a gateway to new possibilities; and the ever-present undo/redo arrows, offering a safety net for your creative endeavors.

Beneath this horizon lies the ribbon—a versatile tapestry of options that unfolds as you navigate through your creation. The toolbar is a collection of tools, each with a purpose. Text, shapes, lines, and images—each element at your fingertips, awaiting placement on the canvas.

As your gaze descends, the canvas stretches before you—a blank expanse ready to embrace your ideas. The gridlines, subtle guides on this digital parchment, assist in precision and alignment, ensuring that your creativity finds its place with accuracy.

The left sidebar, a silent companion, holds the key to structure and flow. Slides, like chapters in a visual narrative, are displayed, inviting you to arrange, rearrange, and orchestrate your story. The slide sorter view, a bird's-eye perspective, allows for a holistic understanding of your presentation's rhythm.

Venturing to the right, the speaker notes emerge—a secret realm where annotations and reminders find a home. Here, your narrative gains depth as you infuse insights and cues for a more immersive presentation experience.

At the bottom, the timeline, a visual heartbeat, unravels the progression of your creation. Each slide, a moment in time, arranged in a chronological dance, awaits your command.

The user interface isn't just a layout; it's a curated space where every element serves a purpose in facilitating your creative expression. An overview isn't a mere glance; it's an invitation to navigate this digital landscape, where each icon, each function, converges to transform your ideas into a visual masterpiece.

- **Setting Up Your First Presentation**

Embarking on the journey of "Setting Up Your First Presentation" is like laying the foundation for a visual symphony. It's not just about creating slides; it's about orchestrating a narrative that captivates and communicates seamlessly. In this initiation, you become the architect of ideas, and the canvas eagerly awaits your touch.

As you enter the realm of Google Slides, the initial encounter is with the blank canvas—a pristine space where your ideas will come to life. The "+ New" button beckons, the gateway to your creative realm. Here, you define the essence of your presentation by choosing a template or embracing the simplicity of a blank canvas.

Selecting a template is an artistic decision. Each template carries a unique vibe, a visual language that aligns with different moods and messages. It's an opportunity to infuse your presentation with personality from the outset, setting the tone for what's to come.

The canvas now transforms into a series of slides, awaiting your content. Adding slides is a symphony of clicks, each one contributing to the crescendo of your narrative. The order matters, and the left sidebar becomes your visual roadmap, allowing you to arrange and rearrange your slides with ease.

Text becomes the brushstroke of your narrative. Each text box is a canvas within a canvas, inviting you to articulate your ideas with precision. Formatting options abound in the toolbar, from font styles to alignment, empowering you to infuse your text with visual impact.

But a presentation is not just about words. Images become the visual melody, and the process of inserting them is a harmonious dance with the "+ Image" option. Your visuals add depth, emotion, and context, elevating your presentation beyond mere words.

Themes and layouts emerge as your artistic palette. Choosing them is not just about aesthetics; it's about the visual structure of your story. Experimentation is encouraged as you explore the myriad options available, tailoring your presentation to resonate with your audience.

Setting up your first presentation is not a tutorial; it's a creative venture. Each decision, from template selection to content arrangement, contributes to the narrative tapestry you're weaving. Your canvas is alive with possibilities, and as you navigate this initiation, you're not just creating slides; you're crafting an experience.

CHAPTER 2
CREATING YOUR FIRST PRESENTATION

- **Choosing a Template**

Choosing a template in Google Slides is akin to selecting the visual tone for your narrative—a decision that sets the stage for your presentation's aesthetic and resonates with your audience. The template gallery unfolds like a curated collection of artistic possibilities, each option offering a unique ambiance for your ideas to flourish.

The "+ New" button is your gateway, and as you enter, the template gallery sprawls before you. Here, you're not just choosing a design; you're selecting the backdrop for your story. The simplicity of a blank slate awaits, but the templates beckon with their preconceived visual identities.

Each template is a visual archetype—a design language that encapsulates a specific mood or purpose. The Business template exudes professionalism, with clean lines and muted tones, while the Creative template bursts with vibrant colors, unleashing a spirit of innovation. Your choice isn't arbitrary; it's a deliberate expression of your presentation's personality.

Hovering over a template is an exploration. It's a preview, a glimpse into the world your audience will step into. The font pairings, color schemes, and overall layout—each element contributes to the template's character. It's not just about aesthetics; it's about aligning the visual language with the essence of your message.

Clicking on a template is a commitment—a declaration of intent. As the template unfolds onto your canvas, it becomes the scaffolding for your ideas. It's not a constraint; it's a foundation that enhances your creativity. The placeholders are placeholders no more; they are prompts, guiding your content into a harmonious coexistence with the chosen design.

But the choice is fluid. Changing your mind is a click away, a testament to the flexibility of Google Slides. The journey of choosing a template isn't a one-time decision; it's a dynamic dialogue between your ideas and the visual landscape. It's an artistic collaboration where your story and the template converge to create a presentation that not only communicates but resonates visually.

- **Adding Slides and Organizing Content**

In the realm of Google Slides, adding slides and organizing content is a choreography of creativity—a dance between structure and expression. The canvas, initially a blank expanse, comes alive with each added slide, and the left sidebar becomes a visual symphony where your narrative takes shape.

The act of adding a slide is a click—a rhythm in the creative process. Whether it's the simplicity of a blank slide or the resonance of a predefined layout, each addition contributes to the fluidity of your presentation. Your canvas transforms into a series of moments, each awaiting your content.

The left sidebar, a navigator in this creative odyssey, unfolds to reveal the slide sorter view. It's not just a list of slides; it's a storyboard of your narrative. Dragging and dropping, you orchestrate the sequence of your story, ensuring a seamless flow that resonates with your audience.

Each slide is a canvas within itself. As you click into the content area, it's not just about text; it's a dialogue with ideas. Text boxes appear, inviting you to articulate your thoughts with precision.

Organizing your content becomes an intuitive process as you arrange and format text effortlessly.

Images are the visual heartbeat, and the process of adding them is a visual dialogue with the canvas. The "+ Image" option opens a portal to your visual library, allowing you to infuse your slides with images that amplify your message. Drag, resize, and arrange—each image finds its place in the narrative.

Layouts become the choreography of your content. Choosing them is not just about structure; it's about visual emphasis. Whether it's a title slide commanding attention or a content slide providing depth, each layout choice shapes the visual language of your presentation.

The toolbar, a versatile ensemble of options, offers alignment, spacing, and arrangement tools. It's not just about placing elements; it's about fine-tuning your composition, ensuring a harmonious balance between text and visuals.

Adding slides and organizing content isn't a mechanical process; it's a narrative composition. Each click, each arrangement, contributes to the storytelling tapestry. It's not just about creating slides; it's about crafting an experience where your ideas seamlessly unfold, resonating with your audience in a visual symphony.

- **Inserting Text and Images**

In the canvas of Google Slides, inserting text and images is a poetic act—a fusion of words and visuals that transforms your presentation into a visual narrative. It's not just about filling spaces; it's about infusing life into your ideas, creating a symphony where text and images dance in harmony.

Text becomes the ink of your narrative. As you click into the text box, the canvas becomes a parchment awaiting your words. Font styles, sizes, and colors unfold in the toolbar, offering a palette for expression. Each keystroke is a stroke of the brush, shaping your ideas with precision and intent.

Organizing text is a rhythm—a dance of bullets, numbering, and indentation. The toolbar becomes your choreographer, offering alignment options that bring order to your textual composition. It's not just about words; it's about the visual cadence they create on the canvas.

Images, the visual melody, weave into this composition seamlessly. The "+ Image" option is an invitation to a visual dialogue. Your image library unfolds, and as you select, drag, and drop, the canvas transforms. Images aren't just adornments; they are visual anchors, enhancing your narrative with depth and emotion.

Resizing and cropping become the nuances of your visual composition. The corners of the selected image invite you to shape and refine, ensuring that each visual element finds its perfect place on the canvas. It's not just about adding images; it's about curating a visual experience.

The arrange tools in the toolbar are your sculptor's tools, allowing you to layer and stack elements with precision. Images behind text, text in front of images—each arrangement contributes to the visual hierarchy of your slide. It's not just about placement; it's about creating focal points and guiding your audience's gaze.

Transitions, a visual crescendo, can be applied to text and images alike. They're not just movements; they're transitions between scenes in your visual story. As you explore the options, the canvas becomes a dynamic stage, and each transition is a cue for your audience to follow.

Inserting text and images isn't a mere act of filling space; it's a narrative composition. Each word, each image, contributes to the visual language of your presentation. It's a delicate balance—a dance where text and images converge to create a presentation that not only communicates but resonates visually.

- **Formatting Text and Objects**

In the canvas of Google Slides, formatting text and objects is a choreography of style—a dance where each element finds its rhythm, creating a visual language that speaks volumes. It's not just about appearance; it's about the deliberate choices that shape the aesthetics of your presentation.

Text, the ink of your narrative, becomes a canvas within itself. As you click into the text box, the toolbar unfolds with formatting options. Font styles, sizes, and colors are not just choices; they are brushstrokes that infuse your words with personality. The canvas becomes a palette, and each formatting decision contributes to the visual tone of your message.

Bold, italics, and underline are the accents—the bold strokes that add emphasis and nuance to your words. The toolbar offers these tools as your editorial instruments, allowing you to punctuate your narrative with visual cues. It's not just about what you say; it's about how you say it.

Alignment becomes the composition—the arrangement of words on your visual canvas. Left, center, right, or justified—the toolbar offers the options to craft the visual cadence of your text. It's not just about organization; it's about creating a visual rhythm that guides your audience through your ideas.

Bullets and numbering are the choreography of lists—a visual sequence that brings order to your content. The toolbar provides these tools as your organizational assistants, helping you structure your information with clarity. It's not just about listing; it's about guiding your audience through a visual hierarchy.

Objects, whether shapes or images, become the sculptures on your canvas. As you click and select, the toolbar transforms into a set of formatting tools. Resize, reshape, and rotate—each action is a stroke that refines the visual composition. It's not just about placement; it's about sculpting the visual landscape.

The fill color and outline options are your painter's palette. Whether it's the backdrop of a shape or the border of an image, these formatting choices add layers to your visual composition. It's not just about objects; it's about creating a cohesive visual experience.

Transparency and drop shadows become the subtleties—the nuances that add depth to your visual elements. As you explore these options, the canvas gains dimension, and your objects become more than shapes; they become visual anchors.

Formatting text and objects isn't a mechanical task; it's a stylistic expression. Each formatting decision, whether applied to text or objects, contributes to the visual language of your presentation. It's a dance of style—a deliberate choreography where each element plays a role in creating a presentation that not only communicates but captivates visually.

- **Using Themes and Layouts**

In the realm of Google Slides, using themes and layouts is akin to composing the visual score of your presentation—a symphony of design choices that harmonize to create a cohesive and captivating visual experience. It's not just about aesthetics; it's about infusing your presentation with a visual identity that resonates with your message.

Themes, the overarching visual motif, set the tone for your entire presentation. As you navigate to the toolbar, the "Slide" menu becomes your portal to a curated collection of themes. Each theme is more than a design; it's a visual language that encapsulates a mood, a purpose, a story waiting to unfold.

Choosing a theme is not a mere selection; it's a deliberate decision that aligns the visual identity with the essence of your message. Whether it's the professionalism of the Business theme or the vibrancy of the Creative theme, your choice becomes the canvas upon which your ideas will dance.

Layouts, the architectural blueprints of your slides, offer a structure for your narrative. The "Layout" option in the toolbar becomes your toolset for visual composition. Title slides, content slides, and section breaks—each layout is a design choice that guides the flow of your presentation.

Selecting a layout is an act of storytelling. The visual hierarchy of title and content, images and text—it's not just about structure; it's about guiding your audience's journey through your narrative. The canvas transforms with each layout, becoming a storyboard that amplifies your message.

Customization is your artistic touch. The "Slide" menu and "Layout" options unfold into opportunities for tailoring your chosen theme to fit your unique vision. Background colors, font styles, and arrangement become your artistic palette, allowing you to infuse your presentation with a personalized touch.

Applying a theme and layout isn't a formula; it's a creative expression. Each choice, each customization, contributes to the visual tapestry of your presentation. It's a visual symphony where themes and layouts converge, creating a harmonious and captivating backdrop for your ideas to unfold.

CHAPTER 3
EDITING AND ENHANCING YOUR PRESENTATION

- **Mastering Slide Transitions**

Mastering slide transitions in Google Slides involves strategically controlling the visual progression between individual slides to enhance the overall flow and engagement of your presentation. The transition options are available in the toolbar, allowing you to dictate how one slide seamlessly transforms into the next.

Google Slides offers various transition effects, each with a distinct visual impact. These effects range from subtle transitions like Fade to more dynamic options like Slide, providing you with choices to match the tone and content of your presentation.

Timing is a crucial element in slide transitions. You have the ability to adjust the duration of each transition, determining how quickly or gradually the transition occurs. This feature allows you to maintain a steady pace, emphasizing key points or maintaining audience interest throughout your presentation.

The "Apply to All Slides" function streamlines the process by enabling you to implement a consistent transition across all slides.

This ensures a uniform visual experience, contributing to the cohesiveness of your presentation.

Effective slide transitions serve a practical purpose—they guide your audience through your content smoothly. The goal is to avoid jarring interruptions and maintain a natural progression that supports, rather than distracts from, your message.

Utilizing the live preview feature enables you to preview how each transition will appear in real-time. This feature allows you to fine-tune your choices, ensuring that the transitions align with your content and contribute positively to the overall presentation experience.

Experimenting with different transitions for various sections of your presentation adds a layer of customization. By tailoring your choices to the nature of the content, you can create a nuanced and engaging visual narrative.

Mastering slide transitions in Google Slides is a practical skill that involves navigating the available options, understanding their effects, and making informed choices to enhance the overall coherence and impact of your presentation.

- **Incorporating Animations**

Incorporating animations in Google Slides is a strategic process that involves adding dynamic movement to individual elements within your presentation. These animations serve to enhance engagement, emphasize key points, and bring a level of visual sophistication to your slides.

The "Slide" menu, accessible from the toolbar, is your gateway to animation options. Here, you can select specific elements—text, images, or shapes—and apply animations to dictate how they appear on the slide.

Entrance animations dictate how an element appears on the slide. Whether it's a simple fade-in or a more dynamic bounce or zoom effect, entrance animations add a layer of visual interest to your content.

Emphasis animations allow you to draw attention to specific elements already on the slide. These animations, ranging from pulsating highlights to bold color changes, enable you to emphasize key information without introducing new elements.

Exit animations control how elements leave the slide. This can be a subtle fade-out or a more dramatic spin or fly-off effect. Exit animations are particularly useful for managing the flow of information and preventing visual clutter.

The Animation Pane, accessible through the toolbar, provides a detailed overview of all applied animations on a given slide. This feature allows you to fine-tune the timing, order, and duration of each animation, ensuring a seamless and cohesive visual experience.

The "Apply to All Slides" option streamlines the process by allowing you to implement a consistent set of animations throughout your presentation. This ensures a uniform visual language and prevents inconsistency in animation styles.

Timing becomes a critical aspect of incorporating animations. Google Slides allows you to specify when each animation should occur, whether it's triggered by a click, automatically after a set time, or in sequence with other animations. This level of control ensures that animations align with your intended pacing.

Live previews enable you to see how animations will unfold in real-time. This feature is invaluable for refining your choices and ensuring that animations complement rather than distract from your content.

Experimentation is encouraged to find the right balance. Applying animations judiciously enhances your presentation, but overuse or inappropriate choices can detract from your message. Thoughtful incorporation of animations contributes to a polished and engaging visual narrative in Google Slides.

- **Customizing Slide Backgrounds**

Customizing slide backgrounds in Google Slides allows you to tailor the visual atmosphere of your presentation, adding a personalized touch to enhance the overall aesthetic. The background customization options, accessible through the toolbar, provide a canvas where color, image, or even gradients can be applied.

The "Slide" menu becomes your hub for background customization. Here, you can choose from a variety of options, including solid colors, gradient fills, images, or even patterns. This flexibility enables you to align the background with the theme and mood of your presentation.

For a simple and clean look, solid color backgrounds offer a palette of choices. This allows you to select a color that complements your content or reinforces your brand identity. The color picker in the toolbar provides precise control over the chosen hue.

Gradients offer a more dynamic background option. Whether it's a subtle blend of colors or a bold transition from light to dark, gradients add depth and visual interest. The gradient tool allows for customization, letting you fine-tune the direction and intensity of the gradient effect.

Incorporating images as backgrounds allows you to infuse your presentation with visuals that align with your message. The "Image" option in the background menu allows you to upload images from your computer, Google Drive, or directly search and insert from the web.

Patterns provide a textured backdrop, introducing subtle visual elements to your slides. These patterns range from simple geometric shapes to intricate designs, offering a unique and stylized background option.

Transparency adjustments in the toolbar enable you to control the opacity of the background, allowing your content to stand out against the backdrop. This feature is particularly useful when using images or patterns as backgrounds.

Applying background customization to specific slides or throughout the entire presentation is facilitated by the "Apply to All Slides" option. This ensures consistency in the visual theme, contributing to a polished and professional presentation.

Live previews allow you to see the immediate impact of your background customization in real-time. This feature is instrumental in refining your choices and ensuring that the background aligns seamlessly with your content.

Experimentation with different background options is encouraged, as it allows you to find the perfect balance that complements your presentation's theme and enhances visual cohesion. Customizing slide backgrounds in Google Slides is a tool for expressing your creativity and reinforcing the overall impact of your message.

- **Adding Audio and Video Elements**

Incorporating audio and video elements in Google Slides amplifies your presentation, transforming it into a dynamic and multimedia-rich experience. The toolbar becomes your command center for seamlessly integrating these elements, enhancing engagement and capturing your audience's attention.

For audio elements, the "Insert" menu becomes your portal. By selecting "Audio," you can upload audio files directly from your computer or link to files stored in Google Drive. This inclusion of audio allows you to underscore key points, set a mood, or provide additional context to your slides.

Once inserted, audio elements are represented by a speaker icon on the slide. Clicking on the icon opens a range of customization options in the toolbar, including volume control, playback settings, and the ability to loop the audio for continuous play.

Video elements are similarly integrated through the "Insert" menu, specifically the "Video" option. You can embed videos from YouTube, Google Drive, or upload directly from your computer. This flexibility ensures that your chosen video content seamlessly integrates with your presentation.

Like audio, video elements offer customization options accessible through the toolbar. You can adjust playback settings, such as starting the video automatically or controlling its volume.

Additionally, you can define whether the video plays within the slide or opens in a separate window.

The positioning and resizing tools in the toolbar allow you to control the placement of both audio and video elements on your slides. This ensures that these multimedia elements enhance rather than overshadow your core content.

The "Format Options" menu provides advanced settings for video elements, allowing you to trim the video duration, add a border, or adjust its transparency. These options give you precise control over how the video integrates into the visual composition of your slide.

Timing becomes a key consideration when incorporating audio and video. You can use the "Format Options" menu to set specific timings, ensuring that these multimedia elements align with the flow of your presentation.

Live previews enable you to see how audio and video elements will behave in real-time. This feature is invaluable for refining your choices and ensuring that these elements seamlessly enhance your narrative.

Experimentation is encouraged to find the right balance. Whether it's incorporating a snippet of music, a voiceover, or a relevant video clip, the addition of audio and video elements elevates your presentation, providing a multi-sensory experience for your audience.

- **Utilizing SmartArt and Charts**

Utilizing SmartArt and charts in Google Slides is a strategic approach to visually communicate complex information, turning data into accessible and engaging visuals. The toolbar becomes your toolkit for transforming raw data into clear, comprehensible graphics.

SmartArt, accessible through the "Insert" menu, allows you to create dynamic visual representations of processes, hierarchies, cycles, and more. By selecting the appropriate SmartArt graphic, you can convey concepts and relationships with ease.

Once inserted, the SmartArt graphic can be customized through the toolbar. The "Format Options" menu provides tools for refining the layout, style, and color scheme of the SmartArt, ensuring it aligns seamlessly with the overall design of your presentation.

Text within SmartArt graphics can be edited directly by clicking on the individual elements. This flexibility allows you to tailor the content to match your specific data or narrative, maintaining a cohesive and clear visual message.

Charts, another powerful tool in the "Insert" menu, enable you to represent numerical data in a visually compelling manner. The chart editor allows you to input data directly or import it from Google Sheets, providing real-time updates as your data changes.

The toolbar offers customization options for charts, allowing you to fine-tune the chart type, style, and color scheme. This ensures that your chart aligns with the overall aesthetic of your presentation.

Data labels, accessible through the toolbar, provide additional context to your charts. You can choose to display labels, values, or percentages, enhancing the clarity of your data representation.

The "Chart & axis titles" option allows you to add titles to your chart, providing context and guiding your audience through the information presented. This customization contributes to the overall narrative flow of your presentation.

Positioning and resizing tools in the toolbar allow you to control the placement of SmartArt and charts on your slides. This ensures that these visual elements integrate seamlessly into your presentation layout.

Live previews enable you to see how SmartArt and charts will appear in real-time. This feature is essential for refining your choices and ensuring that these visuals effectively communicate your data.

Experimentation is encouraged to find the right SmartArt graphic or chart type that best conveys your information. Whether it's illustrating a process, showcasing a hierarchy, or presenting data trends, SmartArt and charts in Google Slides are powerful tools for transforming complex information into visually compelling graphics.

CHAPTER 4
COLLABORATING IN REAL-TIME

- **Understanding Collaboration Features**

Understanding collaboration features in Google Slides opens the door to a world where presentations become a shared canvas, fostering real-time teamwork and seamless communication. The toolbar becomes your control center for collaboration, transforming the traditional presentation into a dynamic, interactive experience.

The "Share" button, prominently positioned in the toolbar, is your gateway to collaboration. By clicking it, you initiate the process of inviting others to view, comment, or edit your presentation. Collaboration becomes a real-time dialogue, breaking down geographical barriers and enabling teams to work together effortlessly.

Collaborators can be added via email, and you have the flexibility to define their level of access—whether it's viewing, commenting, or editing. This granular control ensures that your presentation remains secure while allowing for a spectrum of collaborative interactions.

The comment feature, accessible through the toolbar, becomes the virtual sticky note for collaborative discussions. Comments can be added to specific elements on a slide, providing context, feedback, or suggestions. This feature transforms collaboration from a static process into a dynamic conversation.

Real-time editing is the heartbeat of collaboration in Google Slides. Multiple collaborators can work on the same presentation simultaneously, witnessing changes as they happen. Edits are indicated by color-coded user cursors, creating a visual map of the collaborative landscape.

The "Version history" feature, located in the toolbar, becomes your time machine. It allows you to revisit previous versions of the presentation, track changes, and restore to a specific point. This feature ensures that collaborative iterations are not only dynamic but also reversible.

Notifications, another essential collaboration tool, keep you informed about changes, comments, or invitations. The bell icon in the toolbar becomes your alert system, ensuring that you're always in the loop about the collaborative activity surrounding your presentation.

Real-time presence indicators, showcased by user avatars in the toolbar, provide visibility into who is currently active in the presentation. This feature promotes awareness and facilitates efficient communication among collaborators.

Integration with Google Chat in the sidebar transforms collaboration from asynchronous to synchronous. The ability to chat with collaborators without leaving the presentation enhances real-time communication, fostering a collaborative environment.

Experimentation with collaboration features is encouraged to explore the full potential of shared creativity. Whether it's co-creating a presentation, providing feedback, or engaging in real-time discussions, the collaboration features in Google Slides redefine the traditional presentation, turning it into a collaborative masterpiece.

- **Sharing and Managing Permissions**

Sharing and managing permissions in Google Slides is a strategic process that empowers you to control access, ensuring your presentation remains secure while facilitating collaboration. The toolbar becomes your command center for sharing, allowing you to define who can view, comment, or edit your presentation.

The "Share" button, prominently positioned in the toolbar, initiates the sharing process. By clicking it, you enter the realm of permissions management. Here, you can add collaborators via email and specify their level of access—view, comment, or edit. This granular control ensures that you tailor permissions to match the collaborative needs of your team.

The "Advanced" settings, accessible through the sharing interface, offer additional customization. Here, you can refine permissions further, allowing collaborators to either edit, comment, or only view. Additionally, you can choose whether collaborators can reshare the presentation or access it offline.

Link sharing becomes a flexible option for broader accessibility. By generating a shareable link, you can provide access to a wider audience without individually specifying email addresses. The "Anyone with the link" option ensures that collaborators can access the presentation based on the link's permissions.

The "Copy link" button simplifies the distribution of the shareable link. With a single click, you can copy the link and share it via email, chat, or any communication platform of your choice. This streamlines the process of inviting collaborators and extends the reach of your presentation.

The "Owner" status, displayed in the sharing interface, signifies ultimate control. As the owner, you have the authority to adjust permissions, add or remove collaborators, and manage the overall sharing settings. This status ensures that you retain complete control over the presentation.

The "Viewer," "Commenter," and "Editor" roles provide clear distinctions in terms of permissions. Viewers can observe the presentation, Commenters can add comments, and Editors have full editing capabilities. This hierarchy allows you to tailor access based on the collaborative role of each participant.

Revoking access is a crucial aspect of managing permissions. The "Remove" option in the sharing interface allows you to revoke access for specific collaborators, ensuring that former team members or external parties no longer have access to the presentation.

The "Version history" feature, accessible through the toolbar, adds an extra layer of control. It allows you to track changes, revert to previous versions, and maintain an audit trail of collaborative iterations.

Experimentation with sharing and permissions settings is encouraged to find the balance between collaboration and control. Whether it's collaborating with a small team or sharing broadly, the sharing and managing permissions features in Google Slides provide a robust framework for secure and collaborative presentation creation.

- **Commenting and Reviewing**

Commenting and reviewing in Google Slides transforms collaboration into a dynamic conversation, allowing for feedback, discussion, and refinement of your presentation. The toolbar becomes your hub for facilitating this interactive dialogue, fostering a collaborative environment.

The "Comment" button, prominently displayed in the toolbar, becomes your virtual sticky note. Clicking it allows you to add comments to specific elements on a slide, providing context, feedback, or suggestions. Comments are not just annotations; they become the catalyst for collaborative discussions.

Comments are tied to specific elements, creating a contextual thread. The comment interface, accessible through the toolbar, showcases a timeline of discussions, ensuring that collaborators can easily navigate and contribute to ongoing conversations.

Replying to comments becomes a conversational exchange. The threaded structure of comments allows for a natural flow of discussions, ensuring that feedback is acknowledged, addressed, and refined collaboratively.

Notifications, represented by the bell icon in the toolbar, keep you informed about comments, changes, or invitations. This real-time alert system ensures that you're always aware of the collaborative activity surrounding your presentation.

The "Resolve" option in the comment interface becomes your virtual checkbox. It allows you to mark a comment as resolved once the feedback has been addressed. This feature maintains a tidy workspace, distinguishing between active discussions and resolved issues.

Real-time presence indicators, displayed through user avatars in the toolbar, provide visibility into who is currently active in the presentation. This feature promotes awareness and facilitates efficient communication among collaborators, ensuring that comments are addressed promptly.

The "Chat" feature, integrated into the sidebar, complements commenting by providing a real-time chat interface. Collaborators can engage in synchronous discussions without leaving the presentation, fostering an environment where feedback can be discussed and clarified on the spot.

Live previews enable you to see how comments will appear in real-time. This feature is instrumental in refining your feedback and ensuring that comments align seamlessly with your content.

Experimentation with commenting and reviewing is encouraged to harness the full potential of collaborative feedback. Whether it's providing input on design elements, clarifying content, or discussing strategic decisions, commenting and reviewing in Google Slides create a dynamic and interactive space for collaborative refinement.

- **Co-editing with Team Members**

Co-editing with team members in Google Slides is a seamless and real-time collaboration experience, transforming the traditional notion of solo presentation creation. The toolbar becomes your shared workspace, enabling multiple collaborators to contribute, edit, and refine the presentation simultaneously.

The "Share" button, prominently positioned in the toolbar, initiates the co-editing process. By inviting team members via email, you grant them access to the presentation with the specified level of permission—whether it's viewing, commenting, or full editing rights.

The real-time collaboration feature allows all collaborators to work on the presentation simultaneously. Each user is represented by a color-coded cursor, and changes made by team members are visible in real-time. This dynamic interaction fosters a collaborative environment where ideas flow seamlessly.

The presence indicators, showcased through user avatars in the toolbar, provide visibility into who is actively co-editing the presentation. This feature promotes awareness and facilitates efficient communication, allowing team members to coordinate efforts in real time.

Edits made by collaborators are automatically saved, eliminating the need for manual saving or version control. This ensures that the most up-to-date version of the presentation is accessible to all team members, streamlining the collaborative workflow.

The "Version history" feature, accessible through the toolbar, becomes a safeguard. It allows you to track changes, revert to previous versions, and maintain an audit trail of collaborative iterations. This ensures that even in a co-editing environment, you have the flexibility to review and restore specific states of the presentation.

Comments, another integral part of the co-editing experience, provide a platform for collaborative discussions. Whether it's feedback, suggestions, or clarifications, comments become the virtual sticky notes that facilitate ongoing conversations within the shared workspace.

Notifications, represented by the bell icon in the toolbar, keep all collaborators informed about changes, comments, or invitations. This real-time alert system ensures that the entire team is aware of the collaborative activity surrounding the presentation.

Integration with Google Chat in the sidebar enhances real-time communication during co-editing sessions. The chat interface becomes a space for quick discussions and coordination, enabling team members to communicate without leaving the shared workspace.

Experimentation with co-editing is encouraged to fully grasp the power of collaborative creation. Whether it's brainstorming ideas, refining content, or fine-tuning design elements, co-editing with team members in Google Slides creates a dynamic and synchronized environment for collective presentation development.

- **Version History and Revision Tracking**

Version history and revision tracking in Google Slides serve as your digital archive, providing a transparent and organized view of the evolutionary journey of your presentation. The toolbar becomes your time machine, offering insights into changes made over time and empowering you with the ability to revert to specific states.

The "File" menu, situated in the toolbar, is your gateway to version history. By selecting "Version history" and then "See version history," you unveil a chronological record of edits, additions, and modifications made to your presentation.

Each entry in the version history is timestamped, offering a clear timeline of changes. This allows you to trace the evolution of your presentation, identify key milestones, and understand the collaborative journey that led to its current state.

The "Show changes" option, accessible within the version history, becomes your detective tool. By selecting it, you can visually compare two versions of the presentation, highlighting additions, deletions, and modifications. This feature provides a granular view of specific changes made during the collaborative process.

The "Name current version" option allows you to label specific versions with meaningful titles. This turns the version history into a curated archive, making it easier to identify significant iterations or milestones in the presentation's development.

The "Restore this version" function, available within the version history, is your undo button. It allows you to revert to any previous state of the presentation, ensuring that you can recover content, formatting, or structural elements from specific points in time.

The real-time collaboration aspect seamlessly integrates with version history. Even during co-editing sessions, changes are automatically recorded, providing a comprehensive record of collaborative iterations. This ensures that each team member's contributions are accurately documented.

Notifications, represented by the bell icon in the toolbar, keep you informed about changes and updates. This real-time alert system ensures that you're aware of collaborative activity and can access the latest version of the presentation at any given moment.

Experimentation with version history is encouraged to fully harness its capabilities. Whether it's reviewing collaborative changes, pinpointing specific edits, or restoring to a previous version, version history and revision tracking in Google Slides offer a powerful toolkit for maintaining control and visibility throughout the collaborative creation process.

CHAPTER 5
TIPS AND TRICKS FOR EFFICIENT EDITING

- **Keyboard Shortcuts for Quick Actions**

Keyboard shortcuts in Google Slides are the secret passages, the quick routes that make your navigation and actions more efficient. The toolbar takes a backseat as your fingers dance across the keys, turning complex maneuvers into swift and seamless actions.

1. **Ctrl + C (Cmd + C on Mac):** Copy - Highlight an element, press these keys, and you've captured it on your virtual clipboard.

2. **Ctrl + X (Cmd + X on Mac):** Cut - Similar to copy, but this time you're also removing the selected element.

3. **Ctrl + V (Cmd + V on Mac):** Paste - Take what's on your clipboard and bring it into your presentation.

4. **Ctrl + Z (Cmd + Z on Mac):** Undo - Made a mistake? This is your magic wand to undo the last action.

5. **Ctrl + Y (Cmd + Y on Mac):** Redo - If you change your mind about your change of mind, this brings it back.

6. **Ctrl + B (Cmd + B on Mac):** Bold - Highlight text, press this, and you've added a bold statement.

7. **Ctrl + I (Cmd + I on Mac):** Italicize - Make your text lean a little to the side with this shortcut.

8. **Ctrl + U (Cmd + U on Mac):** Underline - Give your text a line to stand on with this quick action.

9. **Ctrl + A (Cmd + A on Mac):** Select All - Highlight everything in your current slide with this shortcut.

10. **Ctrl + Shift + C (Cmd + Shift + C on Mac):** Copy Formatting - Want to apply the same style elsewhere? Copy the formatting of a selected element.

11. **Ctrl + Shift + V (Cmd + Shift + V on Mac):** Paste Formatting - Apply that copied formatting to another element.

12. **Ctrl + Shift + K (Cmd + Shift + K on Mac):** Insert Link - Select text or an object, hit this shortcut, and link it to a website or another slide.

13. **Ctrl + Enter (Cmd + Enter on Mac):** Start a New Slide - No need to reach for the mouse; press this, and a new slide is born.

14. **Ctrl + Shift + C (Cmd + Shift + C on Mac):** Clear Formatting - Highlight text, press this, and you're back to basics.

15. **Ctrl + Alt + M (Cmd + Option + M on Mac):** Insert Comment - Leave a note for collaborators without interrupting your flow.

16. **Ctrl + Shift + E (Cmd + Shift + E on Mac):** Center Align Text - Ensure your text stands proudly in the middle.

17. **Ctrl + / (Cmd + / on Mac):** Show/Hide Shortcuts - Forget a shortcut? Press this, and a handy menu will remind you.

Experimenting with these keyboard shortcuts can transform your workflow, making your journey through Google Slides swift and effortless.

- **Time-Saving Editing Techniques**

Editing in Google Slides doesn't have to be a laborious task. With a few time-saving techniques, you can breeze through your edits and focus on crafting the perfect presentation. Here are some tricks to keep your editing process efficient:

1. **Ctrl + D (Cmd + D on Mac): Duplicate Slide** - Highlight a slide, press these keys, and voila! You've replicated it, saving you from recreating similar content.

2. **Ctrl + Shift + V (Cmd + Shift + V on Mac): Paste Special** - After copying an element, use this to access a menu where you can choose how to paste it—useful for applying specific formatting.

3. **Ctrl + Alt + (Arrow Keys): Duplicate and Shift** - Select an object, hold these keys, and use the arrow keys to duplicate and shift the object in the desired direction.

4. **Ctrl + Shift + (Arrow Keys): Resize and Shift -** Similar to the duplicate shortcut, use this to resize an object while maintaining its proportions.

5. **Ctrl + K (Cmd + K on Mac): Insert Link -** Highlight text or an object, press these keys, and swiftly link it to a webpage or another slide.

6. **Ctrl + Backspace (Cmd + Delete on Mac): Delete Word -** Position your cursor at the end of a word, and this shortcut will delete the entire word instead of one character at a time.

7. **Ctrl + Shift + C (Cmd + Shift + C on Mac): Copy Formatting -** Click on a formatted object, press this, and apply the same style to another element.

8. **Ctrl + Shift + V (Cmd + Shift + V on Mac): Paste Formatting -** After copying formatting, use this shortcut to apply it to another object.

9. **Ctrl + Alt + E (Cmd + Option + E on Mac): Edit Master -** Quickly access the master slides to make global changes to your presentation's layout and design.

10. **Ctrl + ; (Cmd + ; on Mac): Repeat Last Action -** After performing an action, use this to instantly repeat the last editing command.

11. **Ctrl + Shift + F (Cmd + Shift + F on Mac): Find and Replace** - Need to replace a specific word or phrase throughout your presentation? This shortcut is your time-saving solution.

12. **Ctrl + Shift + 7 (Cmd + Shift + 7 on Mac): Numbered List** - Highlight text and press this to instantly convert it into a numbered list.

13. **Ctrl + Shift + 8 (Cmd + Shift + 8 on Mac): Bulleted List** - Similar to the numbered list, use this to transform text into a bulleted list.

14. **Ctrl + [(Cmd + [on Mac): Indent** - Quickly indent selected text or objects with this shortcut.

15. **Ctrl +] (Cmd +] on Mac): Outdent** - The counterpart to the indent shortcut, use this to remove indentation.

These time-saving editing techniques can turn your editing process into a breeze, leaving you with more time to focus on crafting a compelling and polished presentation.

- **Advanced Formatting Tips**

Take your Google Slides presentations to the next level with these advanced formatting tips. These techniques will help you refine the visual aspects of your slides and create a professional and polished presentation.

1. **Custom Slide Sizes:**

- Go to File > Page Setup to customize the size of your slides. This is useful for creating presentations optimized for different output formats, such as widescreen or standard.

2. **Master Slides for Consistency:**

- Utilize the master slides (View > Master) to establish consistent formatting, such as background styles, fonts, and placeholders. Changes made in the master slides apply to all slides, ensuring a cohesive design.

3. **Format Painter:**

- Found in the toolbar, the Format Painter tool allows you to copy formatting from one element and apply it to another. Double-click the Format Painter to lock it, enabling you to apply the same format multiple times.

4. **Image Masking:**

- Create visually appealing images by using shapes to mask them. Insert a shape, place it over the image, right-click, and choose "Mask image." This technique allows you to control the visible part of the image.

5. **Gradient Backgrounds:**

- Create gradient backgrounds by selecting a slide, going to Slide > Background, and choosing Gradient. Experiment with different color combinations and directions to achieve a modern look.

6. **Image Transparency:**

- Adjust the transparency of images to overlay them seamlessly with other elements. Select an image, go to Format > Adjustments, and use the Transparency slider.

7. **Custom Fonts:**

- Import custom fonts to give your presentation a unique style. Go to the Font menu and choose "More fonts" to access Google Fonts and add them to your presentation.

8. **Drop Shadows:**

- Add depth to objects by applying drop shadows. Select an object, go to Format > Drop shadow, and customize the shadow's color, transparency, and distance.

9. **Line Spacing and Letter Spacing:**

- Fine-tune text appearance by adjusting line spacing and letter spacing. Highlight text, go to Format > Line spacing or Letter spacing, and choose the desired values.

10. **Object Alignment and Distribution:**

- Perfectly align and distribute objects by selecting them, clicking on Arrange in the toolbar, and choosing options like Align or Distribute.

11. **Grouping and Ungrouping:**

- Group related objects together for easier manipulation. Select objects, right-click, and choose "Group." Conversely, you can ungroup them when needed.

12. **Edit Points for Shapes:**

- Refine shapes by editing their points. Right-click on a shape, choose Edit points, and manipulate the anchor points to achieve custom shapes.

13. **Chart Customization:**

- Fine-tune charts by clicking on them, selecting Chart & axis titles in the toolbar, and experimenting with various customization options like colors, labels, and styles.

14. **Animation Customization:**

- Customize animations for individual elements by selecting them, going to Slide > Animation, and adjusting settings like duration, delay, and type.

15. **Object Rotation:**

- Precisely rotate objects by selecting them, clicking on Arrange, and using the Rotate option. Hold down Shift to rotate in 15-degree increments.

These advanced formatting tips provide the tools you need to elevate the visual appeal and cohesiveness of your Google Slides presentations. Experiment with these techniques to create presentations that stand out and leave a lasting impression.

- **Troubleshooting Common Issues**

Encountering issues in Google Slides can be frustrating, but fear not! Here are solutions to common problems to help you troubleshoot and get back to creating stellar presentations:

1. **Unable to Open a Presentation:**

- If you're having trouble opening a presentation, ensure you have a stable internet connection. Try accessing the presentation from a different browser or device. If the issue persists, check if the file is not restricted or blocked.

2. **Slow Performance:**

- If Google Slides is lagging, close unnecessary tabs or applications to free up system resources. Clear your browser cache, restart your browser, or try a different browser for better performance.

3. **Lost Internet Connection During Editing:**

- If you lose internet connectivity while editing, changes made during the offline period may not sync immediately. Once reconnected, click the "Offline" icon (next to the account profile) and choose "Retry syncing."

4. **Formatting Glitches:**

- If you notice formatting issues, such as text misalignment or distorted images, try refreshing the page (F5 or Ctrl + R). Ensure your browser is updated, or try accessing Google Slides in an incognito or private browsing window.

5. **Images Not Loading:**

- If images aren't loading, check your internet connection and try refreshing the page. If the issue persists, ensure the images are in a supported format (JPEG, PNG, GIF) and that they are not corrupted.

6. **Auto-Save Not Working:**

- Auto-save is designed to work seamlessly, but if you suspect it's not, manually save your presentation regularly. Go to File > Save to ensure your changes are saved, especially before closing the presentation.

7. **Missing Fonts:**

- If your presentation contains custom fonts that are not available on another device, Google Slides may replace them. To avoid this, use standard Google Fonts or make sure to share the custom font files with collaborators.

8. **Unable to Insert Videos:**

- Ensure your video is in a supported format (MP4, AVI, MOV) and is hosted on a platform compatible with Google Slides, such as YouTube or Google Drive. Use the "Insert" menu to embed the video.

9. **Collaboration Issues:**

- If collaborators are experiencing difficulties accessing or editing the presentation, check their permissions. Make sure they have the correct sharing settings and are signed in to their Google accounts.

10. **Exporting or Printing Problems:**

- If you encounter issues exporting or printing, try using a different browser. Adjust the print settings to match your preferences, and ensure that your browser's pop-up blocker is not preventing the export.

11. **Unexpected Logouts:**

- If you're unexpectedly logged out, it could be due to issues with your browser's cookies or cache. Clear your browser's cache, restart it, and log back into your Google account.

12. **Issues with Add-ons:**

- If you're experiencing problems with add-ons, disable them temporarily and see if the issue persists. Re-enable them one by one to identify the culprit. Check for updates to ensure compatibility.

If you've tried these troubleshooting steps and the issue persists, consider reaching out to Google Support or consulting the Google Workspace Help Center for more in-depth assistance.

- **Customizing Your Workspace**

Make Google Slides truly yours by customizing your workspace. From themes and layouts to personal preferences, here's how you can tailor your environment for maximum productivity and creativity:

1. **Themes and Color Schemes:**

- Click on "Slide" in the top menu, choose "Change background," and explore different themes and color schemes. Experiment with combinations that match your presentation's tone or your personal style.

2. **Master Slides for Consistency:**

- Use the master slides (View > Master) to set a consistent layout for all your slides. Customize placeholders, fonts, and background elements to create a cohesive design.

3. **Personalized Fonts:**

- Head to the Font menu and choose "More fonts" to access Google Fonts. Select fonts that resonate with your style or match your brand. This will make your presentation distinct and visually appealing.

4. **Custom Slide Sizes:**

- Go to File > Page Setup to define custom slide sizes. This is handy for creating presentations optimized for different platforms or screen dimensions.

5. **Toolbar Arrangement:**

- Rearrange your toolbar for quick access to your most-used features. Click on "View" and choose "Show toolbar" to customize the arrangement based on your workflow.

6. **Customized Thumbnails:**

- In the left sidebar, you'll find thumbnail previews of your slides. Right-click on a slide and choose "Change background" to customize its thumbnail, making it visually distinct.

7. **Grid and Guides:**

- Enable the grid and guides (View > Grid and Guides) for precise alignment of objects. Customize the grid spacing and color to match your preferences.

8. **Image and Video Filters:**

- Click on an image or video, go to Format options, and experiment with filters to enhance or stylize your media. Adjust brightness, contrast, and saturation to achieve the desired effect.

9. **Personalized Templates:**

- Save your customized slides as templates for future use. Go to File > Save as template, and you'll have a personalized starting point for your next presentation.

10. **Custom Slide Transitions:**

- Click on "Slide" in the top menu, choose "Transition," and experiment with different transition effects. Customize the duration and apply consistent transitions to maintain a professional flow.

11. **Custom Thumbnails in Presenter View:**

- If you're using Presenter view, customize the thumbnails for your notes. Right-click on a slide in the Presenter view and choose "Change background" to add visual cues for your speaking points.

12. **Personalized Default Settings:**

- Set your preferred default settings for new presentations. Go to File > Slide > Set up slide, customize the layout, background, and placeholders, and click "Apply to all slides."

13. **Workspace Color:**

- Some extensions or themes allow you to customize the overall color scheme of your Google Workspace. Explore options that align with your preferences.

14. **Keyboard Shortcuts:**

- Customize keyboard shortcuts for specific actions. Go to "Tools" > "Preferences" > "Keyboard shortcuts" to tailor the shortcuts based on your habits.

By personalizing your Google Slides workspace, you create an environment that aligns with your style and enhances your efficiency. Experiment with these customization options to make your presentation creation process a more enjoyable and tailored experience.

CHAPTER 6

PRESENTING LIKE A PRO

- **Rehearsing Your Presentation**

Rehearsing your presentation and setting up Presenter Mode in Google Slides allows you to practice and refine your delivery, ensuring a confident and engaging performance. Here's a guide to help you make the most of these features:

Rehearsing Your Presentation:

1. **Accessing Speaker Notes:**

- In the bottom-left corner of your screen, you'll find the "Speaker notes" section. Use this area to jot down reminders, key points, or cues to guide your presentation.

2. **Presenter View:**

- Click on "Present" in the top-right corner to enter Presenter view. This view allows you to see your slides, speaker notes, and upcoming slides in a clear layout, while your audience sees only the current slide.

3. **Timing Your Presentation:**

- As you rehearse, pay attention to the timing feature in the bottom-left corner. It displays the elapsed time, helping you gauge whether you're pacing your presentation effectively.

4. **Navigating Slides:**

- Use the arrow keys or click on the screen to move between slides. Familiarize yourself with the flow of your presentation, ensuring a smooth transition from one slide to the next.

5. **Testing Slide Transitions:**

- Check how slide transitions occur during your rehearsal. Make sure they align with your speaking points and contribute to the overall narrative flow.

6. **Practicing Interactions:**

- If your presentation includes interactive elements, such as links or buttons, practice interacting with them during the rehearsal. Ensure a seamless user experience.

7. **Adjusting Timing:**

- If you find that your presentation is running too short or too long, consider adjusting the pacing or content. Rehearse until you feel confident in delivering the presentation within the allocated time.

8. **Receiving Feedback:**

- Invite a colleague or friend to join your rehearsal as an audience member. Their feedback can provide valuable insights into your delivery, pacing, and overall presentation effectiveness.

Setting Up Presenter Mode:

1. **Enter Presenter View:**

- Click on "Present" in the top-right corner. This will open your presentation in full-screen mode for your audience, while giving you access to Presenter view.

2. **Adjusting Display Settings:**

- If you're using multiple monitors, click on the gear icon in the Presenter view and select the appropriate display for your audience. This ensures that they see the full-screen presentation while you have control over the Presenter view.

3. **Using Presenter Tools:**

- In Presenter view, you have access to tools like a laser pointer, zoom, and drawing tools. Experiment with these features to enhance your delivery and emphasize key points.

4. **Speaker Notes:**

- Speaker notes are visible only to you in Presenter view. Use this area to glance at reminders or additional information while maintaining eye contact with your audience.

5. **Switching Slides:**

- Navigate through slides using the arrow keys or by clicking on the screen. The audience sees only the current slide, while you have a clear view of the upcoming content.

6. **Exiting Presenter View:**

- To exit Presenter view, press the "Esc" key. This takes you back to the regular editing view in Google Slides.

By rehearsing your presentation and utilizing Presenter Mode, you'll be well-prepared to deliver a polished and engaging talk. Practice, refine, and familiarize yourself with the tools to ensure a confident and effective presentation experience.

- **Customizing Presentation Settings**

Customizing presentation settings and interacting with your audience in Google Slides can elevate your presentation experience. Whether you're tailoring the viewing experience or engaging with your audience, here's how to make the most of these features:

Customizing Presentation Settings:

1. **Accessing Presentation Settings:**

- Click on the gear icon in the top-right corner of the Google Slides interface. This opens the "Settings" menu, where you can customize various aspects of your presentation.

2. **Setting Up Presenter View:**

- In the Settings menu, enable "Presenter view" to access a layout that shows your current slide, speaker notes, and upcoming slides. This is helpful for rehearsing and delivering your presentation confidently.

3. **Adjusting Slide Size:**

- Customize the slide size by going to File > Page Setup. Choose from standard sizes or enter custom dimensions. This is useful if you have specific requirements for your presentation, such as widescreen or custom dimensions.

4. **Enabling Auto-Advance:**

- If you want slides to advance automatically after a certain duration, go to the "Settings" menu and enable "Auto-advance slides." Specify the duration to control the pace of your presentation.

5. **Choosing Presentation Type:**

- In the Settings menu, you can choose between "Present with a speaker" or "Present by yourself." The former allows others to control the presentation, while the latter gives you full control.

6. **Setting Up Q&A:**

- Enable the Q&A feature in the Settings menu to allow the audience to submit questions during the presentation. You can address these questions in real-time or during a dedicated Q&A session.

Interacting with Your Audience:

1. **Enabling Audience Tools:**

- When presenting, click on the audience tools icon (speech bubble) in the bottom-right corner. This opens a menu with options like Q&A, Polls, and Captioning. Enable the tools you want to use.

2. **Q&A Feature:**

- If you've enabled Q&A, audience members can submit questions. You can view and answer these questions in real-time, enhancing interactivity and engagement.

3. **Polling Feature:**

- Conduct polls during your presentation by selecting the "Polls" option in the audience tools menu. Create and launch polls to gather feedback or opinions from your audience.

4. **Captioning Feature:**

- Enable live captions to display spoken words as text on the screen. This is particularly helpful for accessibility and ensuring that all audience members can follow your presentation.

5. **Audience Participation:**

- Encourage audience participation by inviting them to use the Q&A feature or respond to polls. This makes your presentation more interactive and responsive to the needs and interests of your audience.

6. **Monitoring Engagement:**

- Throughout your presentation, monitor audience engagement using the Q&A and Polls tabs. This feedback can guide your presentation and help you tailor it to the audience's interests.

7. **Ending Q&A and Polls:**

- Once you've addressed questions or received sufficient responses, you can end the Q&A or polls session. This allows you to transition smoothly to the next part of your presentation.

Customizing presentation settings and interacting with your audience in Google Slides not only enhances the viewing experience but also fosters engagement and participation. Experiment with these features to create dynamic and interactive presentations that captivate your audience.

- **Handling Q&A Sessions**

Handling Q&A sessions in Google Slides allows you to engage with your audience, address their inquiries, and create a dynamic and interactive presentation experience. Here's a step-by-step guide on how to effectively manage Q&A sessions:

1. **Enable Q&A Feature:**

- Before starting your presentation, go to the Settings menu (gear icon) and enable the Q&A feature. This allows audience members to submit questions during the presentation.

2. **Prompting Audience for Questions:**

- At appropriate points in your presentation, encourage the audience to submit questions using the Q&A feature. Let them know how and when you'll address the questions, whether it's in real-time or at the end of the presentation.

3. **Viewing and Managing Questions:**

- During the presentation, click on the audience tools icon (speech bubble) in the bottom-right corner. Navigate to the Q&A tab to view questions submitted by the audience. Questions may appear in real-time, giving you the flexibility to address them as they come in.

4. **Answering Questions in Real-Time:**

- If you choose to answer questions in real-time, click on a question in the Q&A tab to display it on the screen. Respond verbally or incorporate the question into your presentation, fostering a dynamic and interactive atmosphere.

5. **Dedicating a Q&A Session:**

- Alternatively, you can choose to dedicate a specific portion of your presentation to answering questions. Announce when the Q&A session will begin, pause your presentation, and navigate to the Q&A tab to address the submitted questions systematically.

6. **Moderating Questions:**

- As the presenter, you have the ability to moderate and filter questions. If you receive inappropriate or irrelevant questions, you can choose not to display them to the audience. This ensures a focused and professional Q&A session.

7. **Closing the Q&A Session:**

- When you're ready to conclude the Q&A session, inform the audience that you'll be moving on to the next part of the presentation. Click on the "End Q&A" button to close the Q&A feature and transition seamlessly.

8. **Reviewing Unanswered Questions:**

- After the presentation, you can review any unanswered questions in the Q&A tab. Consider addressing these questions through follow-up communication or incorporating them into future presentations or materials.

9. **Encouraging Follow-Up Communication:**

- If time constraints prevent you from answering all questions during the presentation, encourage the audience to reach out for further clarification or discussion. Provide contact information or direct them to relevant resources.

10. **Expressing Gratitude:**

- Thank the audience for their engagement and participation in the Q&A session. Acknowledge the value of their questions and contributions to create a positive and interactive presentation experience.

Effectively handling Q&A sessions in Google Slides enhances audience engagement, provides valuable insights, and fosters a collaborative atmosphere. Whether addressing questions in real-time or during a dedicated session, the Q&A feature empowers you to connect with your audience and create a memorable presentation experience.

CHAPTER 7

INTEGRATING WITH OTHER GOOGLE WORKSPACE APPS

- **Importing and Exporting Files**

Importing and exporting files in Google Slides allows you to collaborate seamlessly, share your presentations with others, and incorporate content from various sources. Here's a guide on how to efficiently manage the import and export of files:

Importing Files:

Importing Slides from Another Presentation:

1. Open the Google Slides presentation where you want to import slides.
2. Click on "File" in the top-left corner.
3. Select "Import slides" from the dropdown menu.
4. Choose the presentation you want to import slides from.
5. Select the specific slides you want to import.
6. Click on "Import slides."

Importing Images and Media:

1. Open the Google Slides presentation.

2. Click on "Insert" in the top menu.

3. Choose "Image" or "Video" to import media.

4. Select the source of the media (Drive, URL, Upload, etc.).

5. Follow the prompts to import the media into your presentation.

Exporting Files:

Exporting as PowerPoint or PDF:

1. Open the Google Slides presentation you want to export.

2. Click on "File" in the top-left corner.

3. Hover over "Download" in the dropdown menu.

4. Choose the desired export format, such as PowerPoint or PDF.

5. Adjust any export settings if necessary.

6. Click on the preferred option to download the exported file.

Exporting as Image:

1. Open the Google Slides presentation.

2. Click on "File" in the top-left corner.

3. Hover over "Download" in the dropdown menu.

4. Choose "PNG" or another image format.

5. Adjust settings if needed.

6. Click on the desired format to download the image.

Exporting as Video:

1. Open the Google Slides presentation.

2. Click on "File" in the top-left corner.

3. Hover over "Download" in the dropdown menu.

4. Choose "Video" to export as a video file.

5. Adjust video settings if necessary.

6. Click on "Export" to generate and download the video file.

Collaborating with Microsoft PowerPoint:

1. Open the Google Slides presentation.

2. Click on "File" in the top-left corner.

3. Select "Download."

4. Choose "Microsoft PowerPoint (.pptx)."

5. Open the downloaded file in Microsoft PowerPoint to collaborate across platforms.

Tips for Efficient Importing and Exporting:

- **Maintain Compatibility:**

- When importing from or exporting to other formats, ensure compatibility by reviewing the formatting and layout to avoid any discrepancies.

- **Consider File Size:**
- Be mindful of file sizes, especially when exporting as images or videos. High-resolution images and lengthy videos may result in larger file sizes.
- **Check Links and Media:**
- When importing, ensure that links and embedded media are functional. When exporting, double-check that hyperlinks and media are preserved in the exported file.
- **Collaborate in Real-Time:**
- Leverage Google Slides' real-time collaboration features to work seamlessly with others. Share the presentation and collaborate simultaneously.

By mastering the import and export features in Google Slides, you can integrate content seamlessly, collaborate effectively, and share your presentations in various formats to meet your specific needs.

- **Collaborating with Google Docs and Sheets**

Collaborating with Google Docs and Sheets and embedding Google Slides in websites can enhance your productivity and reach. Here's how to seamlessly integrate these tools into your workflow:

Collaborating with Google Docs and Sheets:

Embedding Google Docs:

1. Open the Google Docs document you want to embed.

2. Click on "File" in the top-left corner.

3. Select "Publish to the web" from the dropdown menu.

4. In the "Publish to the web" dialog, click on the "Embed" tab.

5. Choose the display options, such as the size of the embedded document.

6. Copy the generated embed code.

7. Paste the embed code into the HTML of your website or online platform.

Collaborating in Real-Time:

1. Open your Google Slides presentation.

2. Click on the "Share" button in the top-right corner.

3. Enter the email addresses of collaborators or choose "Copy link" to share a link.

4. Set permissions (view, comment, or edit) for each collaborator.

5. Click "Send" to invite collaborators.

Commenting and Suggesting Changes:

1. With collaborators added, they can add comments by selecting text or objects and choosing "Comment" from the toolbar.

2. Suggestions can be made by selecting text or objects, right-clicking, and choosing "Suggesting."

Linking to Google Sheets:

1. Open your Google Slides presentation.
2. Go to the slide where you want to add the link.
3. Highlight the text or object you want to turn into a link.
4. Click on the "Insert" menu and choose "Link."
5. Select "Sheets" and choose the spreadsheet you want to link to.

Embedding Google Slides in Websites:

Publishing to the Web:

1. Open your Google Slides presentation.
2. Click on "File" in the top-left corner.
3. Select "Publish to the web" from the dropdown menu.
4. Choose the options for the presentation (start slide, auto-advance, etc.).
5. Click "Publish."
6. Copy the provided embed code.

Embedding in Websites:

1. Open your website's HTML editor.

2. Paste the copied embed code where you want the presentation to appear.

3. Save and publish your website to make the embedded Google Slides presentation visible.

Customizing Embed Options:

1. When publishing to the web, click on the "Embed" tab to customize options like slide size and auto-advance.

2. Adjust settings to tailor the embedded presentation to your preferences.

Tips for Effective Collaboration and Embedding:

- **Version Control:**
- Utilize version history in Google Slides to track changes and revert to previous versions if needed.
- **Communication:**
- Use comments and suggestions in Google Slides for effective communication with collaborators.

- **Accessibility:**
- Consider the accessibility of embedded documents on your website. Ensure that users can navigate and comprehend the content.
- **Privacy Settings:**
- Set appropriate privacy settings when collaborating to control who can access and edit your documents.
- **Responsive Design:**
- Ensure that embedded Google Slides presentations on your website have a responsive design for optimal viewing on various devices.

By seamlessly integrating Google Docs, Sheets, and Slides into your collaboration and presentation workflows, you can create a more efficient and interactive experience for yourself and your audience.

- **Integrating with Google Meet**

Integrating Google Slides with Google Meet and syncing with Google Drive can streamline your workflow and enhance collaboration. Here's how to seamlessly connect these Google Workspace tools:

Integrating with Google Meet:

1. **Start a Google Meet Session:**

- Open Google Meet and start a new meeting.
- Alternatively, join an existing meeting.

2. **Access Google Slides:**

- During the meeting, click on the "Present Now" button at the bottom of the screen.
- Choose "A Chrome tab" or "Your entire screen" to share your Google Slides presentation.

3. **Select the Google Slides Tab:**

- If you chose to share a Chrome tab, select the tab with your Google Slides presentation.
- Click "Share."

4. **Navigate Slides in the Meeting:**

- Once your presentation is shared, navigate through your slides as usual.
- Meeting participants will see the slides in real-time.

5. **Use Presenter View:**

- If you're using Presenter view in Google Slides, only the presentation content will be visible to participants, while you can view your speaker notes and upcoming slides.

6. **End Presentation:**

- When you're done presenting, click on the "Stop presenting" button in Google Meet.

Syncing with Google Drive:

Uploading to Google Drive:

1. **Save Your Presentation:**

- Open your Google Slides presentation.
- Click on "File" in the top-left corner.
- Choose "Save" or "Save a copy" to ensure changes are saved.

2. **Access Google Drive:**

- Open Google Drive in your browser.

3. **Upload the Presentation:**

- Drag and drop the saved presentation file into the Google Drive window.
- Alternatively, click on the "+" button and choose "File upload" to select your presentation.

Collaborating and Editing:

1. **Share from Google Drive:**

- Right-click on your presentation file in Google Drive.
- Choose "Share" to collaborate with others.

2. **Real-Time Collaboration:**

- When collaborating, changes made by you or collaborators in Google Slides are automatically synced to the Google Drive file in real-time.

3. **Access Anywhere:**

- Your Google Slides presentation is accessible from any device with internet access through Google Drive.

4. **Version History:**

- In Google Drive, right-click on the presentation file.
- Choose "Version history" to see past versions and revert to earlier states if needed.

Offline Access:

1. **Enable Offline Mode:**

- In Google Drive, click on the gear icon in the top-right corner.
- Select "Settings."

- Enable offline mode to access your presentations without an internet connection.

2. **Offline Editing:**

- When offline mode is enabled, you can edit your Google Slides presentations and changes will sync once you're back online.

Tips for Seamless Integration:

- **Use Google Drive for Centralized Access:**
- Store your Google Slides presentations in Google Drive for centralized access, collaboration, and version control.
- **Utilize Google Meet for Remote Collaboration:**
- Use Google Meet for remote presentations, meetings, and collaborative discussions, seamlessly integrating with Google Slides.
- **Set Sharing Permissions:**
- When collaborating, set appropriate sharing permissions in Google Drive to control who can view or edit your presentations.
- **Familiarize with Presenter View in Meetings:**

- If using Presenter view in Google Slides during Google Meet sessions, familiarize yourself with how it appears to participants and adjust as needed.

By integrating Google Slides with Google Meet and syncing with Google Drive, you create a cohesive and efficient workflow for collaborative presentations and document management.

CHAPTER 8

ADVANCED FEATURES AND FUTURE TRENDS

- **Exploring Advanced Animation Options**

Unlock the full potential of your Google Slides presentations by exploring advanced animation options and incorporating add-ons for extended functionality. Here's a guide to help you take your presentations to the next level:

Exploring Advanced Animation Options:

1. **Access Animation Pane:**

- Click on the slide where you want to apply advanced animations.
- Go to the "Slide" menu and select "Transition."

2. **Customize Transition Effects:**

- In the Transition pane, customize the transition effects, duration, and other options.
- Click on "Apply to all slides" if you want consistent transitions.

3. **Add Entrance and Exit Animations:**

- Go to the "Slide" menu and select "Animation."

- Choose "Add Animation" and select entrance or exit animations for specific objects.

4. **Adjust Animation Timing:**

- Click on an animated object, go to the "Slide" menu, and select "Animation."

- Choose "Animation options" to adjust timing, order, and other settings.

5. **Use Motion Paths:**

- Select an object, go to the "Slide" menu, choose "Animation," and add a motion path.

- Customize the path by dragging the endpoints or using predefined paths.

6. **Animate Text and Objects Individually:**

- Click on a text box or object, go to the "Slide" menu, and choose "Animation."

- Add entrance, exit, or emphasis animations to individual elements.

7. **Combine Animations:**

- Experiment with combining multiple animations on a single object for dynamic effects.

- Use the Animation Pane to manage the order and timing of animations.

8. **Animate Charts and Graphs:**

- Select a chart or graph, go to the "Slide" menu, choose "Animation," and add appropriate animations.
- Customize the animation options to highlight specific data points.

9. **Apply Emphasis Animations:**

- Use emphasis animations to draw attention to specific elements on your slides.
- Adjust the intensity and timing to create subtle or impactful effects.

10. **Utilize Advanced Transition Options:**

- Explore advanced transition options like morph transitions for seamless object movements between slides.
- Experiment with different easing options to control the acceleration and deceleration of animations.

Using Add-ons for Extended Functionality:

1. **Accessing Add-ons:**

- Click on the "Add-ons" menu in Google Slides.

- Choose "Get add-ons" to explore and install additional functionalities.

2. **Adding Icons and Illustrations:**

- Use add-ons like "Icons by Noun Project" to easily insert high-quality icons into your presentation.
- Enhance visual appeal and convey ideas effectively.

3. **Enhancing Data Visualization:**

- Explore add-ons like "Chartify" to create advanced charts and visualizations directly within Google Slides.
- Improve the representation of complex data.

4. **Creating Interactive Quizzes:**

- Integrate add-ons like "FormLimiter" or "Flubaroo" to create interactive quizzes within your presentation.
- Collect responses and provide instant feedback.

5. **Embedding Live Web Content:**

- Use add-ons like "LiveSlides" to embed live web content, such as websites and social media feeds, directly into your slides.
- Keep your audience engaged with real-time updates.

6. **Generating QR Codes:**

- Install add-ons like "QR Code Generator" to quickly create QR codes for links, contact information, or other data.
- Enhance interactivity and provide easy access to additional resources.

7. **Creating Timelines and Gantt Charts:**

- Explore add-ons like "Office Timeline" to easily create timelines and Gantt charts within Google Slides.
- Communicate project timelines and milestones effectively.

8. **Enabling Audio Narration:**

- Use add-ons like "Talk&Comment" to add voice narration to your slides.
- Enhance your presentations with personalized audio explanations.

9. **Implementing Image Editing Tools:**

- Install add-ons like "Pixlr Editor" to access advanced image editing tools directly within Google Slides.
- Enhance and customize images seamlessly.

10. **Collaborative Brainstorming:**

- Explore collaborative add-ons like "MindMeister" to enable real-time brainstorming and mind mapping within your presentation.
- Foster collaborative creativity.

By mastering advanced animation options and leveraging add-ons for extended functionality, you can create visually stunning and interactive presentations that captivate your audience. Experiment with these features to discover new ways to express your ideas and enhance the overall impact of your Google Slides presentations.

- **Accessibility Features in Google Slides**

Enhance the inclusivity of your presentations by utilizing accessibility features in Google Slides, and stay ahead of the curve by keeping up with updates and new features. Here's a guide to help you make your presentations more accessible and stay informed:

Accessibility Features in Google Slides:

1. **Alt Text for Images:**

- Select an image, go to the "Format" menu, and choose "Alt text."
- Add descriptive alt text to ensure accessibility for individuals using screen readers.

2. **Heading Structure:**

- Use the "Title" and "Subtitle" placeholders for slide titles and subtitles.
- Create a logical heading structure using the heading options in the toolbar.

3. **Reading Order:**

- Arrange content in a logical reading order.
- Use the "Order" option in the "Arrange" menu to adjust the reading order.

4. **Accessible Fonts and Colors:**

- Choose readable fonts and maintain sufficient color contrast for text and background.
- Avoid relying solely on color to convey information.

5. **Keyboard Shortcuts:**

- Familiarize yourself with keyboard shortcuts for navigation and actions.
- Press "Ctrl + /" to access the list of keyboard shortcuts.

6. **Screen Reader Support:**

- Ensure compatibility with screen readers by structuring content logically.

- Test your presentation using screen reader tools to identify and address accessibility issues.

7. **Slide Titles and Descriptions:**

- Provide meaningful slide titles and descriptions for each slide.
- This helps individuals navigate and understand the context of each slide.

8. **Use of Lists and Headings:**

- Utilize bulleted or numbered lists for organized content.
- Implement heading styles for sections and sub-sections.

9. **Descriptive Hyperlinks:**

- Make hyperlinks descriptive and provide context.
- Avoid generic terms like "click here" and use meaningful link text.

10. **Accessible Tables:**

- If using tables, ensure they are simple and have clear headers.
- Use the "Table" menu to add headers and structure data effectively.

Keeping Up with Updates and New Features:

1. **Visit Google Workspace Updates:**

- Regularly check the Google Workspace Updates blog for announcements and updates related to Google Slides.

2. **Explore the Help Center:**

- Visit the Google Slides Help Center for comprehensive guides, tutorials, and information on new features.

3. **Follow Google Workspace on Social Media:**

- Stay informed about updates by following Google Workspace on Twitter and other social media platforms.

4. **Join Google Workspace Communities:**

- Participate in Google Workspace user communities and forums to exchange information and stay updated on the latest features.

5. **Attend Webinars and Workshops:**

- Attend webinars and workshops hosted by Google to gain insights into new features and best practices.

6. **Enable Beta Features:**

- If you're comfortable with testing new features, consider enabling beta features in your Google Slides settings to access experimental functionalities.

7. **Feedback and Suggestions:**

- Provide feedback and suggestions through the Google Workspace platform to contribute to the improvement of Google Slides.

8. **Explore Early Access Programs:**

- Check for early access programs that allow you to try out upcoming features before they are officially released.

9. **Subscribe to Newsletters:**

- Subscribe to newsletters or mailing lists related to Google Workspace updates to receive regular notifications.

10. **Collaborate with Google Slides Users:**

- Engage with other Google Slides users, share tips, and discuss new features in online communities or forums.

By prioritizing accessibility features in Google Slides and staying informed about updates and new features, you ensure that your presentations are not only inclusive but also take advantage of the latest tools and functionalities available in the platform.

- **Future Trends in Presentation Technology**

Here are some anticipated future trends in presentation technology:

1. **Augmented Reality (AR) and Virtual Reality (VR):**

- **Immersive Experiences:** AR and VR technologies will offer immersive experiences, allowing presenters to transport audiences to virtual environments.

- **Interactive 3D Content:** Presenters might utilize 3D models and simulations for a hands-on exploration of concepts, products, or data.

2. **Artificial Intelligence (AI) Integration:**

- **Real-time Insights:** AI algorithms could provide real-time insights, such as sentiment analysis of the audience, enabling presenters to adapt their delivery.

- **Automated Content Generation:** AI might assist in generating presentation content, creating slides, and suggesting improvements based on user preferences.

3. **Interactive and Touchless Interfaces:**

- **Gesture Control:** Gesture control interfaces will enable presenters to navigate slides or interact with content using natural hand movements.

- **Voice Commands:** Voice-activated commands will become more sophisticated, allowing presenters to control slides and access information verbally.

4. **Dynamic and Real-Time Collaboration:**

- **Cloud Collaboration:** Cloud-based platforms will facilitate real-time collaboration, enabling team members to work on presentations simultaneously from different locations.

- **Versioning and Tracking:** Advanced collaboration tools will include robust version control and tracking features to monitor changes and contributions.

5. **Blockchain for Security and Authentication:**

- **Secure Data Sharing:** Blockchain technology will enhance the security of shared presentations, ensuring the integrity and authenticity of content.

- **Access Control:** Smart contracts on the blockchain may govern access control, allowing presenters to define permissions for various users.

6. **Personalization and Adaptive Content:**

- **User Profiling:** Presentation tools will use user profiling to understand preferences, adapting content dynamically based on individual preferences.

- **Feedback-driven Adaptations:** AI algorithms might analyze audience feedback during presentations, adjusting content in real-time to meet audience expectations.

7. **Integration with Wearable Devices:**

- **Smart Glasses Integration:** Wearable devices like smart glasses could offer a hands-free presentation experience, displaying slides directly in the user's field of vision.

- **Biometric Feedback:** Wearables might collect biometric data to gauge audience engagement and tailor presentations accordingly.

8. **Data Visualization Advancements:**

- **Machine-generated Visualizations:** Machine learning algorithms will assist in creating complex visualizations, turning raw data into compelling and easy-to-understand graphics.

- **Interactive Infographics:** Data presentations will evolve with interactive infographics, allowing audiences to explore datasets dynamically.

9. **Environmental Sustainability:**

- **Energy-efficient Presentations:** Presentation tools will prioritize energy efficiency, reducing the environmental impact of running multimedia-rich presentations.

- **Paperless Options:** A strong push toward paperless presentations will contribute to sustainability efforts.

10. **Enhanced User Experience Design:**

- **Intuitive Interface Design:** User interfaces will be designed for seamless navigation and a more intuitive user experience.

- **Personalized Workflows:** Presentation tools will adapt to users' preferences, offering personalized workflows and features.

11. **Holographic Presentations:**

- **Hololens Integration:** Integration with holographic displays, such as Microsoft HoloLens, could bring holographic elements into presentations for a futuristic and visually stunning experience.

- **Spatial Presentations:** Presenters might utilize spatial computing to arrange holographic elements in 3D space for enhanced storytelling.

12. **Gamification Elements:**

- **Interactive Quizzes and Challenges:** Gamification features will include interactive quizzes, challenges, and rewards, making presentations more engaging and educational.

- **Progress Tracking:** Presenters may use gamified elements to track audience participation and progress throughout the presentation.

Keeping abreast of these evolving trends will empower presenters to leverage cutting-edge technologies and create more impactful and engaging presentations in the future.

CONCLUSION

In conclusion, "Google Slides For Beginners: The Complete Step-By-Step Guide To Learning How To Create, Edit, Share And Collaborate On Presentations" serves as an indispensable resource for individuals embarking on their journey into the dynamic realm of digital presentations. Throughout the book, we've navigated the foundational principles and intricacies of Google Slides, unraveling its vast potential for creating compelling, collaborative, and visually stunning presentations.

As we delved into the core chapters, readers gained a comprehensive understanding of the basics, from the fundamental features of Google Slides to the rationale behind choosing this platform for presentation creation. The exploration of the user interface, setting up presentations, and selecting templates provided a solid groundwork for crafting presentations with both efficiency and creativity.

The subsequent chapters ventured into the heart of presentation creation, covering the insertion of text, images, and multimedia elements. We delved into the nuances of formatting, exploring themes and layouts, ensuring that readers not only learn the how but also comprehend the why behind each design choice.

The book took an in-depth journey into advanced features, unraveling the magic of slide transitions, animations, and customization options. By demystifying these advanced techniques, readers gained the expertise to captivate their audience through visually appealing and dynamic presentations.

Furthermore, we explored the collaborative features of Google Slides, illuminating the pathways to seamless sharing, managing permissions, commenting, reviewing, and co-editing with team members. Understanding version history and keyboard shortcuts provided valuable insights for efficient collaboration and quick actions.

The book then extended its reach beyond the creation process, delving into the practicalities of importing and exporting files, collaborating with Google Docs and Sheets, and embedding presentations in websites. By mastering these aspects, readers gained a holistic understanding of how Google Slides integrates seamlessly into various workflows.

As the journey unfolded, we didn't just stop at the present features of Google Slides but peeked into the future trends of presentation technology. The anticipation of augmented reality, artificial intelligence, and interactive interfaces hinted at a future where presentations transcend traditional boundaries, becoming immersive and adaptive experiences.

Lastly, we emphasized the importance of accessibility features in making presentations inclusive and discussed strategies for staying ahead of the curve through continuous learning, exploring new features, and embracing emerging technologies.

In essence, this book is not just a guide; it's a companion for those venturing into the dynamic world of digital presentations. Whether you're a student, professional, or someone seeking to enhance their communication skills, the knowledge imparted in these pages empowers you to not only master Google Slides but also to elevate your storytelling and collaboration abilities in an ever-evolving digital landscape. May your presentations be impactful, your collaborations seamless, and your journey in the realm of presentations truly transformative. Here's to your success in crafting presentations that leave a lasting impression.

www.ingramcontent.com/pod-product-compliance
Lightning Source LLC
La Vergne TN
LVHW022012200926
848481LV00007B/2360
* 9 7 9 8 2 2 3 1 0 5 6 5 7 *